MICR

The Benefits of Bacteria

Revised and Updated

W/D

Robert Snedden

www.heinemann.co.uk/library
Visit our website to find out more information about Heinemann Library books.

To order:
☎ Phone ++44 (0) 1865 888112
▤ Send a fax to ++44 (0) 1865 314091
💻 Visit the Heinemann Bookshop at www.heinemann.co.uk/library to browse our catalogue and order online.

First published in Great Britain by Heinemann Library, Halley Court, Jordan Hill, Oxford OX2 8EJ, part of Harcourt Education. Heinemann is a registered trademark of Harcourt Education Ltd.

Editorial: Clare Lewis
Design: Joanna Hinton-Malivoire
Picture research: Ruth Blair
Production: Sevy Ribierre

Originated by Chroma Graphics (Overseas) Pte. Ltd
Printed and bound in China by Leo Paper Group

ISBN 978-0-431-09344-4 (hardback)
11 10 09 08 07
10 9 8 7 6 5 4 3 2 1

ISBN 978-0-431-09494-6 (paperback)
12 11 10 09 08
10 9 8 7 6 5 4 3 2 1

British Library Cataloguing in Publication Data
Snedden, Robert
Microlife: The Benefits of Bacteria – 2nd edition
616'.014
A full catalogue record for this book is available from the British Library.

Acknowledgements
The publishers would like to thank the following for permission to reproduce photographs:
M Abbey p. **15**, M Bond p. **9**, Dr J Burgess pp. **6**, **10**, **13**, **20**, T Buxton p. **11**, CNRI p. **31**, Corbis/Reuters p. **35**, EM Unit, VLA p. **7**, Favre, Felix/Jerrican p. **23**, S Fraser p. **38**, Corbis/Owen Franken p. **24**, P & T Leeson p. **26**, Dr K Lounatmaa p. **14**, Prof. P Motta, Dept of Anatomy, University La Sapienza, Rome p. **17**, Novosti p. **42**, C Nuridsany & M Perennou p.**32**, A Pasieka pp. **5**, **33**, Rosenfeld Images Ltd p. **21**, Science Photo Library pp. **16**, **29** (AJ Photo/Hop Americani), S Stammers p. **19**, St Mary's Hospital Medical School p. **28**, US Department of Energy p. **45**, J Walsh p. **22**, Dr M Wurtz/Biozentrum, University of Basel p. **30**; Still Pictures: P Gleizes p. **8**.

Cover photograph:
Coloured transmission electron micrograph of a section through a *Proteus* bacteria.
Reproduced with permission of Science Photo Library.

The Publishers would like to thank Dr Puran Ganeri and Anna Claybourne for their comments in the preparation of this title.

Every effort has been made to contact copyright holders of any material reproduced in this book. Any omissions will be rectified in subsequent printings if notice is given to the publishers.

Any words appearing in the text in bold, **like this**, are explained in the Glossary.

Contents

Introduction

Think of **bacteria** and you probably think of germs, disease, and illness, and the importance of washing your hands before meals. It is true that some bacteria, and other **micro-organisms**, can cause serious illnesses, but most bacteria are not harmful. In fact, without bacteria, there would be no life on Earth as we know it.

Death and decay

Bacteria that live in soil break down, or decompose, the remains of dead plants and animals. In the process, they make available **nitrates** and other important substances used by living plants as they grow. These pass to the animals that eat the plants. Of course the bacteria do not do this to be helpful, it is just the way in which they obtain the energy they need to survive.

Working on the inside

Some bacteria colonize the digestive systems of humans and other animals. From the bacteria's point of view this is a good move. They get a reasonably safe home and regular deliveries of food. Coincidentally, they also perform a valuable service in exchange. Bacteria in the stomachs of grass-eating animals, such as cattle, break down cellulose (the indigestible material that forms the stiff walls of plant **cells**). Bacteria in our intestines break down food and release **nutrients** that would otherwise pass through our bodies and be lost as waste.

Down in the mouth

Some kinds of bacteria even live in pits at the back of your tongue. They get their energy by breaking down one form of nitrogen **compound** into another that can help to kill the harmful bacteria that cause cavities in your teeth.

Without the benefit of the microbes in their guts, cows would get little nourishment from the grass they eat.

Making use of microbes

We have found many surprising ways to turn the extraordinary properties of bacteria and other micro-organisms to our advantage. We use bacteria to ferment milk and to make cheese, butter, and yoghurt. Yeasts, tiny microscopic **fungi**, are used to make bread rise and to make alcoholic drinks such as beer and wine.

Just as larger plants and animals compete with each other for food and space so, too, do **microbes**. By employing the weapons that bacteria have **evolved** over millions of years to gain an advantage over each other, we can use one bacterium to combat the disease caused by another. We can even make use of the ability of bacteria to live in some of the most hostile places on the planet to run chemical processes in a more environmentally friendly way.

No one knows how many species of bacteria there might be, or what abilities they might have. We may just be scratching the surface of our relationship with these marvellous micro-organisms. But one thing to remember is that bacteria are only doing what they have to do for their own good. If we, or any other organism, can benefit from this it is by chance and not design.

A *Lactococcus lactis* bacterium. This is one of the micro-organisms that is involved in making yoghurt.

The clean-up crew

All living things produce waste in one form or another and eventually living things die. Imagine what the world would be like if all the waste and remains of once-living organisms were simply left to pile up. Fortunately, there is a group of organisms called decomposers. They play a vital part in the living world by feeding on this organic waste. Many of the most important decomposers are micro-organisms such as bacteria and fungi.

Decomposers

A food chain shows the path that energy takes through an **ecosystem**. At the start of every food chain there are the producers, such as green plants or microscopic **algae**, trapping energy from the sun, or bacteria obtaining energy from chemical reactions. This energy can be used by other organisms, called consumers, further along the chain. They eat the producers or other consumers. The decomposers are the last link in the chain.

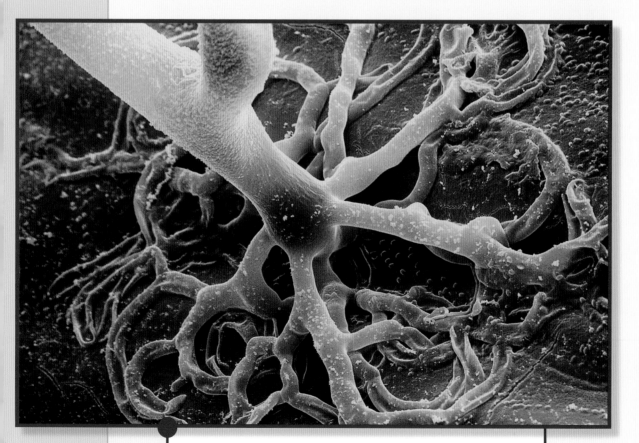

Part of a bread-mould fungus. The microscopic fungus drifts in the air until it lands on a suitable foodstuff and starts to grow.

What sets decomposers apart from other consumers is that they break down the food they consume into **inorganic nutrients**. This releases the nutrients back into the soil, water, and air, so they can be used again. If there were no decomposers there would eventually be no life at all as all of the available nutrients would become locked up in waste and dead bodies.

Breakdown squad

Not all decomposers are micro-organisms. The earthworm is a well known and obvious example of one of the larger decomposers, as are the larvae of flies and other insects that feed on dead animals. The earthworm is at the start of the decomposition process, breaking down dead organic matter into smaller fragments. At this point the microscopic decomposers, the bacteria and fungi, take over. They break the fragments down even more, releasing the nutrients that will be used again by plants. There are billions of bacteria in every handful of fertile soil.

Decomposers in you

Decomposers can be found wherever there is organic matter. There are even decomposing bacteria in your intestines that help you to extract nutrients from your food. They carry on the digestive process by releasing essential nutrients from the food we eat. This is an example of a **symbiotic** relationship – one that helps both organisms. The bacteria find food and shelter in your intestines and you get vitamins and other nutrients that would not otherwise have been available to you.

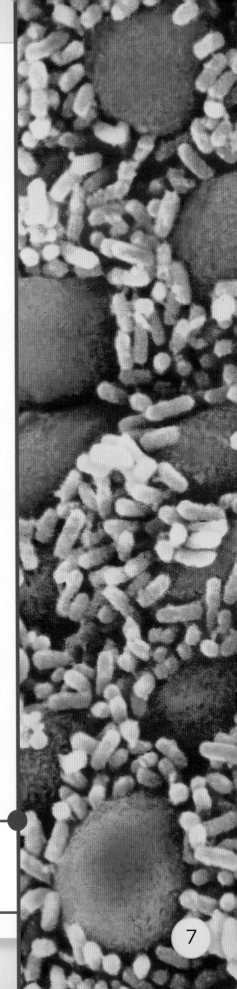

Escherichia coli bacteria growing inside a human intestine. Everyone has these colonies of bacteria inside them.

Sewage disposal

Every day humans produce over 5 billion kilograms (11 billion pounds) of waste. Add to this all of the waste being produced by other animals and it amounts to a massive waste disposal problem. Luckily for us, we can make use of countless billions of micro-organisms, including millions of different species of **protists**, fungi, and **bacteria**, to help deal with the problem.

Faeces feeders

Animal manure is easily broken down by micro-organisms. In fact, micro-organisms are at work on the manure even before it leaves the animal! Around a third of the weight of manure is made up of bacteria such as *Escherichia coli*, a common bacterium that is found in the guts of humans and other animals.

Dirty work

As we have seen, decomposers are constantly at work recycling natural waste. However, the fact that many of us now live in large towns and cities has created a waste problem that bacteria alone cannot solve – they cannot recycle the waste fast enough. We have had to find ways of using bacteria to process our waste more efficiently.

Animal manure, like this, contains nitrogen, phosphorus, and potassium. The action of micro-organisms releases these important **nutrients** into the soil.

Septic tanks

A septic tank is an underground tank in which billions of microbes slowly break down sewage. Septic tanks contain mainly anaerobic bacteria, those that live without oxygen. The process of breaking down sewerage produces a great deal of gas, more than half of which may be methane. This can be collected and used as a fuel. The final solid product can be used as a fertilizer. Anaerobic bacteria are now also being used to break down some types of household waste, to help save space in landfills.

Spraying and filtering

Larger quantities of sewage are treated using aerobic bacteria, those that need oxygen to live. One form of treatment involves spraying the sewage on to a thick layer of crushed rock. Micro-organisms, including protists and bacteria, cling to the rock surfaces, forming a **biofilm**. Some of the materials in the sewage are broken down into simpler substances by the micro-organisms and large numbers of bacteria are consumed by the protists in the biofilm.

In another method, the waste water is mixed with microbes and air to make "activated sludge". The microbes soak up the waste particles and release clean water and carbon dioxide gas.

A more efficient method is to use a biological **aerated** filter. This consists of a submerged bed of fine granular material – again coated with a biofilm. The sewage is trickled through the granular material and air is pumped in at the base of the bed. This air flow allows bacteria that break down ammonia in the wastes to grow and become established.

Filter beds in a sewage plant. Bacteria in the gravel of the bed break down sewage, helping to make it harmless.

The nitrogen cycle

Nitrogen is essential for all forms of life. All **proteins** and the **nucleic acids**, **DNA** and **RNA**, contain nitrogen. This means that it is vital that the supply of nitrogen to the living world is maintained. The movement of nitrogen around the environment is one of the planet's great natural cycles and bacteria are involved at every stage.

An ocean of nitrogen

We are surrounded by a vast ocean of nitrogen. Nitrogen gas makes up 78 per cent of the air we breathe. However, for the majority of organisms, nitrogen is quite unusable in this form as it does not readily combine with other substances.

Nitrogen fixation

Some bacteria can make use of atmospheric nitrogen. Using nitrogen gas to form nitrogen-containing compounds, such as ammonia and **nitrate**, is called nitrogen **fixation**. Around 90 per cent of the world's annual supply of fixed nitrogen is supplied by bacteria. A small amount of nitrogen is fixed by lightning flashes and the rest is supplied in the form of artificial fertilizers produced industrially by chemical fixation.

Atmospheric nitrogen is fixed mainly by free-living soil bacteria such as *Azotobacter*, by *Rhizobium* bacteria, which associate with the legume family of plants, and by **cyanobacteria**, which are found free-living in soil and water and also sometimes in association with plants or fungi.

These are nodules on the root of a pea plant caused by the presence of *Rhizobium* bacteria, which convert atmospheric nitrogen into a form the plant can use.

Plant partnerships

All plants need nitrogen to ensure their growth, but there are none that can make use of atmospheric nitrogen directly. *Rhizobium* bacteria form symbiotic relationships with leguminous plants, a group that includes clover, alfalfa, beans, and peas, and with a few others, such as alders. The bacteria live inside swellings, called nodules, that form on the roots of the plant in response to the presence of the bacteria. The bacteria obtain food from the plants and, in turn, supply the plants with nitrogen compounds that the plant can use to make proteins. Up to 225 kilograms (500 pounds) of nitrogen per hectare of land may be fixed annually by the action of these bacteria.

Energy hungry

Bacteria use a lot of energy to fix nitrogen. Between a tenth and a third of the energy a leguminous plant produces through **photosynthesis** may go to the bacteria in the root nodules.

Nitrogen relationships

Many cyanobacteria can also fix atmospheric nitrogen. Some types of cyanobacteria form symbiotic relationships with fungi and with plants such as ferns. For example, the cyanobacterium *Anabena* becomes associated with a small water fern called *Azolla*. *Azolla* is found widely, especially in the paddy fields of China and other Asian countries where rice is grown. As the rice plants grow they shade the water ferns, which die and release their nitrogen for the rice plants to take up. Rice plants that grow with the water ferns give substantially better yields than those grown without – thanks to the cyanobacteria.

Cyanobacteria are important in the efficient farming of rice, the staple food of almost half the world's population.

Nitrogen conversions

Decomposing animal remains and animal wastes contain organic nitrogen. However, this form of nitrogen is just as unusable as atmospheric nitrogen for most organisms. Many different types of micro-organism convert the nitrogen-containing waste into ammonia. Some micro-organisms use the ammonia for making their own proteins and some of this leaks into the surrounding soil where it can be used by other bacteria and by plants.

Nitrification

Nitrosomonas and other bacteria **oxidize** the ammonia to nitrites. Other soil bacteria such as *Nitrobacter* oxidize the nitrites to nitrates. This process is called nitrification. The nitrates can then be taken up again by green plants. Most plants get nearly all of their nitrogen in this form and use it to make proteins.

Nitrosomonas and *Nitrobacter* exist in what is known as a commensal relationship. This is a relationship in which one benefits and the other neither benefits nor suffers. *Nitrobacter* is dependent on *Nitrosomonas* for its supply of nitrites but *Nitrosomonas* does not need *Nitrobacter*.

Denitrifying bacteria

Another group of micro-organisms, known as denitrifying bacteria, complete the nitrogen cycle. They can convert nitrates back into nitrogen gas. This process is called denitrification and it occurs only in the absence of oxygen. It does not generally take place in well-cultivated soils. The denitrifying bacteria get their energy by breaking down both the nitrogen compounds excreted by living animals and the nitrogen compounds produced by decaying organic matter.

Upsetting the balance

Every year, humans fix vast amounts of nitrogen for use in industry and agriculture. Unfortunately, such large-scale nitrogen production may be affecting the natural nitrogen cycle. Natural denitrification by bacteria may not be able to keep pace with the amounts of nitrogen compounds being produced.

If nitrates get into lakes and rivers the result can be **eutrophication**. This is an explosive growth in the population of bacteria and other micro-organisms, which thrive on the nitrates. The sheer numbers of micro-organisms use up most of the oxygen in the water, making it uninhabitable for fish and other larger organisms.

Fertilizer running into this river from surrounding fields has caused it to become choked by **algae** and bacteria.

Living with microbes

Billions of bacteria live inside your intestines. They provide humans with a vital service, supplying us with essential vitamins and helping us to digest food. The bacteria living in our bodies also keep harmful bacteria at bay, preventing them from gaining a foothold on "their" territory.

You are not alone ...

There are more bacteria cells in and on your body than there are cells making up your body. In fact your body's cells are outnumbered by about a hundred to one!

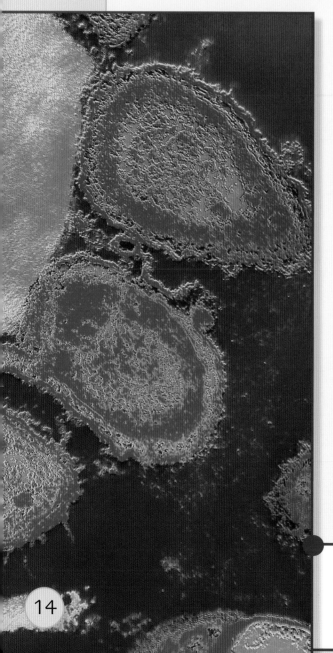

Microdigesters

Bacteria and other micro-organisms play an important part in the lives of plant-eating animals. About 50 per cent of the material of a plant is made of cellulose. In fact, cellulose is the most common organic substance on the planet. However, plant-eating animals cannot digest this tough material. They need help from micro-organisms.

A cow, for example, has a section of stomach, called the rumen, that is home to a huge range of micro-organisms which break down the plant matter the cow eats. They include a type of bacteria called methanogens, which release the gas methane. Methane belched out by cows adds to the greenhouse effect, heating the Earth by preventing heat from escaping. Farmers can reduce the amount of methane their cows produce by giving them high-quality food.

Bacteria in the rumen of a cow. The picture shows plant material in the process of being broken down by the bacteria (red).

14

Team termite

Termites feed on wood and some species cause serious damage in buildings because they consume the wooden structures. However, the termites cannot digest the wood. They are able to eat sound wood only because of the protists that live in their guts. The protists engulf particles of wood consumed by the termite and break them down. These protists may make up as much as a quarter of the termite's body weight. Termites deprived of their protistan partners lose the ability to survive on a diet of good wood, although they can still get by on decaying wood.

A dual organism

These protists are found nowhere else but in the guts of termites. Both organisms are absolutely reliant on each other. The micro-organisms can digest the wood but cannot gather it; the termites can gather the wood but cannot digest it. This is a true partnership, or symbiosis, where both partners gain. It is almost possible to think of the termite and protist as a single wood-consuming organism.

A number of the protist *Triconympha campanula*. These organisms inhabit the guts of termites where they break down the wood the termite eats.

Mouth microbes

In the mouth of every adult human there are more than 400 different species of micro-organism, most of which are bacteria. Billions and billions of them grow on every available surface and tucked into every little crack and crevice. The number of bacteria in your mouth could be greater than the number of people on Earth. Some are harmful, some are neither good nor bad and some may actually do you a lot of good.

What a mouthful!

The mouth has been called the body's equivalent of a tropical rainforest because it is warm and wet and has a huge number of things living there!

Fighting food germs

Recently it has been discovered that bacteria living in our mouths may protect us against other potentially harmful bacteria such as *Salmonella*.

When we eat foods high in nitrates, such as leafy greens and root vegetables, the amount of chemicals called nitrates in our saliva increases. Bacteria living at the back of the tongue take some of the oxygen from the nitrates and use it to convert them from nitrate to nitrite. When the nitrite is swallowed, it reacts with stomach acid to make nitric acid. This powerful chemical can kill bugs that cause food poisoning and diseases, helping to protect us from illness.

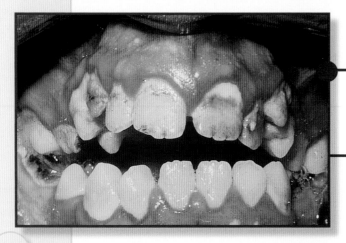

The build up of bacteria on poorly cared-for teeth can cause tooth decay and gum disease.

Unidentified bacteria growing on the surface of a human tongue. Most of the bacteria in your mouth are harmless.

Many bacteria are not harmed by stomach acid alone. The formation of nitric oxide is a valuable additional line of defence against disease-causing microbes.

Fighting decay

The nitrite-forming bacteria have been found living in the mouths of humans, pigs, pigeons, rabbits, and goats, as well as rats. It seems likely that these bacteria play a part in preventing tooth decay. The bacteria that cause tooth decay by producing acids that dissolve tooth enamel are resistant to their own acids. A combination of acid and nitrite will kill them however. The rural Yi, Bai, and Tai peoples of Yunnan, a province of China, suffer almost no tooth decay or stomach cancer. Their diet consists almost entirely of vegetables, many cured in nitrite, and small amounts of preserved meats.

Fungal relationships

It is all too easy to see fungi as agents of destruction. For example, dry rot is a type of fungus that can cause a lot of damage in buildings. It causes timber to become brittle and crumble into powder. Although this may be a nuisance in buildings, it is an important part of the natural recycling process. For example, when a tree is injured it becomes infected with fungi and decays. If there were no decomposer fungi to clear the dead wood from the forests there would eventually be no room for new trees to grow.

Fungi return organic material to the soil, keeping it fertile. They also help to maintain soil structure. Some fungi produce glue-like substances that bind soil particles together. This creates **pores** in the soil, allowing air and water to filter down to plant roots and soil organisms.

Mycorrhizal fungi

Of all the relationships between plants and fungi one of the most important is the one that involves mycorrhizal fungi. "Mycorrhiza" means fungus-root, and refers to the symbiotic relationships between certain soil fungi and the tiny feeder roots of many plants. With the exception of the growing tips, the plant roots become encased in a sheath of fungal tissue. Inside the sheath fungal threads penetrate the plant root.

Fungi growing on the forest floor help to break down dead leaves and wood, recycling the nutrients they contain.

This is called the "chicken-of-the-woods" fungus. It is edible and is considered a delicacy in Germany.

A great many fungal **filaments** branch out from each mycorrhiza and absorb nutrients from the soil, such as phosphorus and nitrogen. This is passed on to the plant. Effectively, the fungi increases the roots' contact with the soil by between 100 and 1,000 times. Mycorrhizae also give some protection from **disease agents** and drought. In return, the fungus, which cannot produce food itself, gets carbohydrate food from the plant.

Fungi and forests

Mycorrhizal fungi are of crucial importance to the well-being of forests. The fungi take up minerals from decaying leaves on the forest floor, ensuring that nutrients are quickly and efficiently recycled. Many of the toadstools and mushrooms you may see on a walk in the woods are actually the fruiting parts of the mycorrhizal fungi associated with the trees.

Robin hood fungi

It has recently been discovered that mycorrhizal fungi will actually transport nitrogen away from nitrogen "rich" plants that have nodules with *Rhizobium* bacteria to "poor" plants that do not. Plants that do not have bacteria to fix nitrogen for them can be made to grow taller and healthier by planting them next to those that do.

Yeast

Yeasts are one of the most useful micro-organisms. These single-celled fungi have been used for centuries to **ferment** the sugars of rice, wheat, barley, and corn to produce alcoholic drinks.

Saccharomyces cerevisiae, commonly known as baker's or brewer's yeast. This organism is used to brew beer and make bread rise.

Yeasts multiply by budding or by dividing and splitting into two new cells. When placed in a sugar solution the population of yeast will start to grow at a great rate as they consume the sugar, converting it into carbon dioxide and alcohol. Yeasts are also found in soil and salt-water, where they play an important part in the decomposition of plants and algae.

Bread

Yeast is used in bread-making as a raising agent for dough. The best-known and most commercially important yeast is *Saccharomyces cerevisiae*. The bread many of us eat today is very different from the first bread ever made which was flat and heavy. The bread that we eat most often is baked from fermented dough, which contains bubbles of carbon dioxide. The bubbles expand when the dough is heated and the bread rises, becoming light and airy. Left alone, dough will ferment naturally. However, this would take a long time so a baker adds yeast to the dough to speed up the fermentation process.

The ancient Egyptians may have been the first to discover the possibilities of yeast. Some yeast cells may have accidentally landed on some unbaked dough, which was then left long enough for an effect to become apparent.

Drug testing

At the beginning of 1999 researchers at Stanford University in the United States said they had found a way to use yeast to see how certain drugs work. They hoped that this might offer a cheap and easy test for compounds to fight cancer, and to make new **antibiotics** and other drugs.

The method they used works by deleting some genetic information from the yeast to make it weaker, and then exposing it to the drug. By deleting particular **genes**, the researchers could work out which genes the drugs had an effect on.

Yeast is also used to manufacture drugs. Pseudoephedrine, for example, a drug used in decongestant medicines, is made by fermenting a special strain of yeast cells mixed with other chemicals. Researchers at the University of California at Berkeley are now working on ways to use yeast to make artemisinin, an anti-malaria drug. This method may eventually help to ensure malaria medicines can be made much more cheaply.

A busy bread production line in a commercial bakery. Without yeast, bread would not rise properly. Flat breads, such as the tortilla and the chapatti, are made without yeast.

Down at the dairy

Bacteria are used to make some of the most familiar of our foodstuffs, such as yoghurt, butter, and cheese.

Yoghurt is a fermented, slightly acidic food made from milk. Yoghurt is usually made from concentrated milk that is soured by the bacterium *Lactobacillus bulgaricus*. A number of bacteria may be used in butter-making and in cheese-making.

Mass-processed yoghurt is made by heating concentrated milk to about 90°C (194°F) for a few minutes, then cooling it to about 44°C (111°F) and adding a **culture** of *Lactobacillus bulgaricus* and *Streptococcus thermophilus*. These two micro-organisms together produce the required acidity and flavour.

Healthy bacteria

During the late 19th century, Elie Metchnikoff, a Russian biologist who worked at the Pasteur Institute in Paris, saw that certain people in the Balkans, for whom yoghurt was a staple part of their diet, seemed to be healthier and live longer. He suggested that the numbers of harmful bacteria in the intestines were being kept down by *Lactobacilli* from the yoghurt.

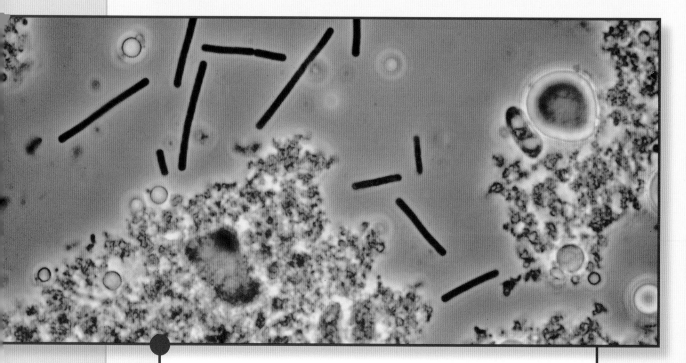

The thin, black rods in this photograph are *Lactobacillus bulgaricus* bacteria, which are found in live yoghurt.

His theory was called into question by other bacteriologists who felt that conditions inside the intestine would not suit the *Lactobacilli* and would stop them from becoming well established.

A yoghurt cure?

However, around a hundred years after Metchnikoff put forward his ideas, scientists are testing yoghurt bacteria such as *Lactobacilli* to see if they really are good for the bowels. Studies suggest that they can improve conditions such as irritable bowel syndrome, and can reduce the number of harmful bacteria in the bowel. Treatments based on *Lactobacilli* and other bacteria could eventually replace antibiotics for some diseases, reducing the problem of antibiotic resistance.

Cheese-making

Cheese is one of the oldest and most nutritious foods we eat. Cheese-making equipment dating from 2000 BC has been found. It is believed that the first cheese was produced accidentally, probably through the habit of carrying milk in pouches made from animal stomachs. The bacteria in the milk and the digestive juices from the stomach worked together to form first a curd and then a crude cheese. Most cheese is formed by the **coagulation** of milk by rennet (the digestive **enzyme** in the stomach of a calf) or similar enzymes. The different types of cheese produced depend on the type of milk used and on the bacteria used in the ripening process – usually *Lactococcus* and *Lactobacillus*.

Bacteria are used to help curdle milk in cheese making.

Fermentation

Certain micro-organisms, such as yeast and some bacteria, can exist in the absence of oxygen. Such organisms are called anaerobes. An anaerobe is an organism that obtains all the energy it needs from food without the use of oxygen. Some bacteria not only cannot use oxygen, they are even poisoned by it. The chemical process by which living cells break down **glucose** in the absence of oxygen to obtain part or all of the energy they need is called fermentation.

Fermenting muscles

Plants and animals can also obtain energy by fermentation. When you exercise hard the cells of your muscles cannot get oxygen quickly enough to obtain energy through ordinary respiration and they fall back on fermentation.

Acid or alcohol

The way humans ferment glucose and the way, for example, yeast does, is exactly the same except for one small difference. When fermentation takes place in your muscle cells, lactic acid is produced. It is the build-up of lactic acid that makes your muscles feel stiff and sore after exercise. When yeast cells ferment glucose, the sugar molecules are converted to alcohol.

Grapes being crushed to make wine. Fermentation occurs when the yeast and sugars mix together.

Wine and vinegar

Beer, wine, and cheese production and several other commercial processes involve fermentation by different types of yeast, bacteria, and fungus moulds. Yeasts are naturally present on the skins of grapes. These come into contact with the grape sugars when the grapes are crushed and fermentation begins naturally. Cultured yeasts are sometimes added to the mix to help fermentation.

Vinegar is produced when bacteria continue the fermentation process. They break down the alcohol produced from sugar by the fermenting yeast to give acetic acid, or vinegar. Soy sauce is fermented with the fungus *Aspergillus soyae*.

Germ theory

Brewer's yeast was used for brewing beer and fermenting grapes and other substances to produce wines and mashes to make distilled spirits, long before the process of fermentation was scientifically understood.

It was the French chemist Louis Pasteur (1822–1895),who first demonstrated that fermentation was dependent on living organisms. Previously it was thought that fermentation was a purely chemical process and that micro-organisms were the result of the process rather than the cause of it. In his *History of Lactic Acid Fermentation*, published in 1858, Pasteur stated that specific kinds of fermentation were caused by the activities of specific micro-organisms. He also said that every disease was caused by a particular microbe, or germ. In this way, the study of fermentation led to the germ theory of disease.

The great French scientist Louis Pasteur is shown here towards the end of his life. His work on fermentation led to the germ theory of disease.

Bioprospecting

Large pharmaceutical companies need new drugs to win the battle against old diseases and to fight new diseases. To find new chemicals that could be used in drugs, they scour the natural world, searching for unusual microbes and the substances they produce. This is called bioprospecting.

Tree treatment

The Pacific yew tree is an important natural source of a potent drug, paclitaxel, which is used to treat certain cancers, such as breast cancer. The tree actually produces the substance to combat moulds. The amount of the drug that can be obtained from each tree is too small to meet demand, and obtaining it kills the tree. It is possible to make the drug chemically, but this is expensive. However, a fungus has been found that grows on the Pacific yew and produces the drug itself.

Perhaps 30 to 50 different fungi grow on a single limb of the yew tree. Many of these microbes, called endophytes, receive nutrients from the tree and in turn give it protection from disease-carrying bacteria or fungi. One of these fungi appears to make the anti-cancer chemical on its own, even when grown apart from the tree. The ability to do this probably gives it an advantage in competition with other microbes. Scientists are still looking at ways of making paclitaxel more cheaply, using the fungus instead of the tree.

Fungus flavouring

One of the first chemicals to be mass produced from fungi was citric acid, which is now used to flavour soft drinks and foods. The acid was originally extracted from citrus fruits such as lemons and limes. In 1917, however, a chemist named James Currie realized that it could be made more cheaply using fungi.

Searching for natural cures

Researchers are interested in discovering other plant-associated microbes that make compounds with medicinal value. For example, the National Cancer Institute in the United States collects 1,000 samples of fungi and **algae** each year, as well as 700 marine organisms and 3,000 plant samples from tropical rainforests throughout the world.

Buried treasure

Ivermectin is a product of a soil bacterium. It can combat **parasitic** worm infections in humans and animals better than any other known substance, paralysing the worms by blocking the transmission of nerve signals. A drug used to lower levels of **cholesterol** by blocking the body's production of this substance was also found in a soil sample. There might literally be wonders in the dirt beneath our feet.

The trunk of a Pacific yew tree. The anti-cancer drug paclitaxel can be extracted from the bark of the tree. Because the tree is rare scientists are looking for other ways to obtain paclitaxel, including from the fungi that grow on the tree.

Antibiotics

The first clue that drugs to combat illness might come from microscopic organisms emerged in 1928, when Alexander Fleming noticed that a mould had invaded a petri dish upon which he was growing a culture of bacteria. In the areas where there were specks of green mould the bacteria had disappeared.

Against life

The effect the mould had on the bacteria was "antibiosis" (against life), a word coined in the 19th century to describe a type of natural competition among species. Fleming tested the mould on a range of bacteria and found that it killed some disease bacteria, but not all of them. He identified the mould as *Penicillium notatum*, a similar mould to that which grows on stale bread, and named the substance it produced "penicillin".

This is the petri dish in which Fleming first noticed that mould seemed to prevent bacteria from growing.

Folk wisdom?

A traditional folk remedy for dealing with infections was to place a piece of mouldy bread on the affected part.

The antibiotic era

It was Dr Selman Waksman, a Russian-born American microbiologist who first used the term "antibiotic" in 1945. The discovery of penicillin was the beginning of the antibiotic era in which medical scientists around the world searched for newer and more effective antibiotics. Doctors today have about a hundred antibiotics to choose from. Some are known as broad-spectrum antibiotics, which means that they are effective against a wide range of bacteria, while others are specific to a single strain of bacteria.

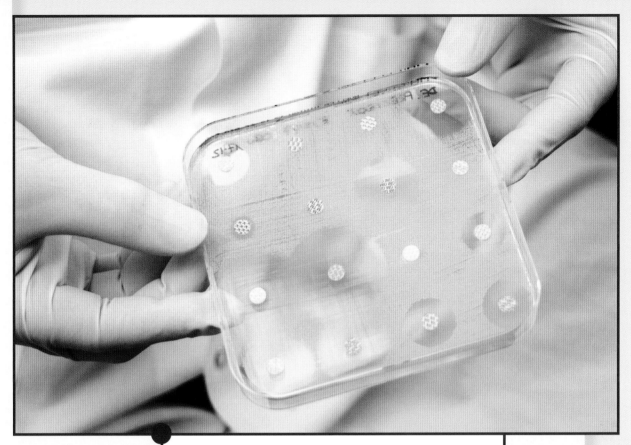

Antibiotic drugs (discs) are being tested on colonies of *Staphylococcus* bacteria (yellow), which have been grown in a petri dish.

Fighting resistance

Increasingly, bacteria have become resistant to the antibiotics we use. This means that drugs that easily destroyed bacteria in the past can no longer do the job. Common bacteria such as *Staphylococcus* can be resistant to the most powerful antibiotics we have.

Streptogramins

The streptogramins are a new class of antibiotics to be introduced in the last 20 years. The first one was discovered in a soil sample from Argentina by researchers searching for new medicinal compounds. When resistance to antibiotics became a problem, streptogramins began to be produced on a large scale and used to treat infections. However, there are also signs that some bacteria are becoming resistant to streptogramins.

One against the other

The increasing resistance of disease-causing bacteria to antibiotics is a problem that medical science has to find an answer to. One possible solution might lie in using **bacteriophages – viruses** that attack bacteria.

Discovering bacteriophages

Felix d'Herelle, a bacteriologist at the Pasteur Institute in Paris, was investigating an outbreak of the disease dysentery in 1917 when he found something that attacked the dysentery bacteria. He believed it to be a virus that was parasitic on bacteria. He called the virus a bacteriophage.

He suspected he might have discovered something that could be used to fight infection. At first his claims were not taken seriously because it seemed extraordinary that microscopic bacteria should themselves be infected by something tinier still. In the 1930s bacteriophages were actually on sale for a while as treatments for dysentery, typhoid, and other illnesses. However, the results were unconvincing and the rise of antibiotics soon pushed bacteriophage treatment into the background.

Miniature attackers

A typical bacterium is about a thousandth of a millimetre across, and a bacteriophage is about 40 times smaller than that. Today we have electron microscopes, a tool not

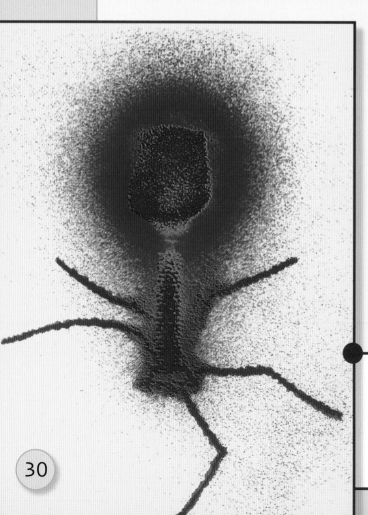

A T4 bacteriophage, a type of virus that attacks only bacteria. T4 viruses specifically attack *E.coli* bacteria and are found in sewage and polluted water.

available to d'Herelle, that can reveal them to us. They look something like microscopic lunar landers with angular heads, long tails, and spindly legs, which they use to cling to the surface of a bacterium. When a bacteriophage makes contact with a suitable bacterium it uses its tail to make a channel through which it shoots its genes into the bacterium. There, the viral genes take control of the bacterium turning it over to the production of more viruses. Within a short time a fresh fleet of viruses burst from the bacterium. The bacterium is left damaged beyond repair and it soon dies.

Phage therapy

Today, antibiotic-resistant bacteria such as *Staphylococcus*, a common cause of infections in hospitals; *Streptococcus*, the cause of scarlet fever, pneumonia and the so-called "flesh eating" infections; and the tuberculosis bacterium, have turned the attention of scientists again to the use of bacteriophages. Unlike antibiotics, bacteriophages only target specific bacteria. Antibiotics can often wipe out good bacteria as well as bad. However, the fact that the bacteriophage is so specific makes it essential to match virus and bacterium exactly when carrying out treatment. As yet bacteriophages have not been found for all bacterial infections, but bacteriophage treatment, known as phage therapy, is used successfully to treat infections suffered by burns victims.

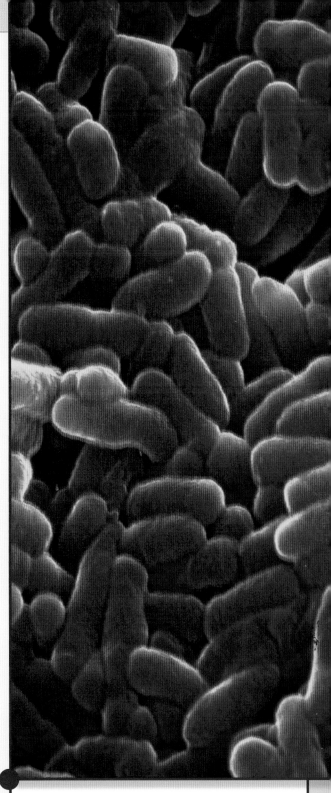

Mycobacterium tuberculosis, the bacteria responsible for tuberculosis. A bacteriophage that attacked this bacterium would be of great benefit.

Biological control

Biological control means using one type of organism to control the numbers or activities of another. It takes advantage of the natural competition between organisms, even at a microscopic scale, to combat pests and diseases that affect domestic animals and crops.

The safer solution

The advantage of biological control is that it tends to be safer than the alternative – the use of chemical pesticides. A typical way of using micro-organisms, or the **toxins** they produce, is to kill or discourage insect pests of crop plants. The bacterium *Bacillus thuringiensis* is an important bioinsecticide that is employed all over the world against a number of pests that affect a variety of crops. Some strains of this bacterium produce toxins that will kill mosquitoes, and efforts are being made to develop an insecticide that can be used to combat diseases spread by mosquitoes, such as malaria and yellow fever.

One problem with biocontrols is in finding organisms that are robust enough to be taken to where they are needed and then multiply enough to do the job efficiently. If at all possible it is best to recruit an organism that is native to the area being treated.

The bioinsecticides include baculoviruses – a group of viruses that cause disease in caterpillars, a major agricultural pest.

Taking the toxins

Genetic engineers have created new strains of crop plants with built-in insecticides by inserting bacterial toxin genes into the plant **chromosomes**. This has the advantage of keeping insect pests under control without exposing other plants and wildlife to insecticide sprays. There are concerns that the insects will eventually become resistant to the toxins and so scientists continue to look for other possibilities. One group of toxins that might eventually be used comes from the bacterium *Photorhabdus luminescens*. This bacterium produces proteins that are effective against a wide range of common insect pests.

Micro-encapsulation

A new technology called micro-encapsulation could help useful viruses, bacteria, and other environmentally-friendly biopesticides compete with traditional chemical pesticides. Encapsulation involves mixing the microbes with a material, such as corn flour, that has been treated to enable it to absorb water. The corn flour-microbe mixture is added to water and then dried and the microbes become entrapped in protective particles so small they can barely be seen. This allows the biopesticides to be dusted on to crops.

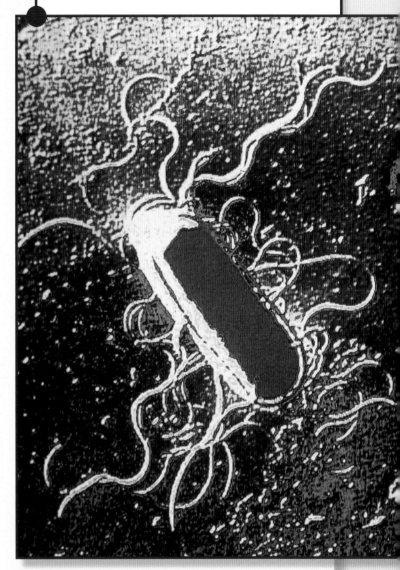

Bacillus thuringiensis. These bacteria are harmless to humans, so they can be used on crops close to harvest time, when it would be too dangerous to use chemical pesticides.

Genetic engineering

Genetic engineering involves the use of biochemical techniques to change the **hereditary** material, or **genes**, of cells. Genes are made of deoxyribonucleic acid, or **DNA**, and genetic engineering includes snipping out bits of DNA and transferring them from one cell to another. This allows changes to be made to the characteristics of an organism that could not be achieved by simple cross-breeding.

Plasmid transfers

Much of the work in transferring genes has been done with bacteria. The genetic information of a bacterium is contained in a single, large DNA molecule called its **chromosome**. Small circular segments of DNA, separate from the main chromosome, are also found in bacteria. These are called **plasmids**. It is possible to take plasmids from one cell and introduce them into another. For example, *Escherichia coli*, a common bacterium found in the digestive systems of many animals, contains a plasmid that gives it resistance to the antibiotic tetracyclin. *E. coli* cells that lack this resistance can be treated chemically to make them take up plasmids from other cells. In this way the *E. coli* cells too become resistant.

Enzyme scissors

It is not possible to slice off pieces of DNA using a conventional blade. It is done using various enzymes known as nucleases or restriction enzymes. These are produced by bacteria as a defence against bacteriophages, the viruses that attack them. The bacteria fight back by using nucleases to cut up the viral DNA. Scientists can use these enzymes to break up molecules of DNA.

The pieces of DNA are then joined using a type of enzyme called a ligase, which repairs breaks in DNA. Scientists use nucleases and ligases to make **hybrid** plasmids, by joining pieces of plasmid from two different bacteria species.

Bactoadium?

Genes from a toad were the first animal genes to be introduced into bacteria. They were joined to plasmids from *E. coli*. The clones that resulted had toad DNA as well as that of the bacterium.

Transgenic organisms

It is now possible to transfer genes from one animal to another, or from an animal to a plant. The DNA may be injected directly into a fertilized egg, or a virus may be used to carry the gene with it as it invades a cell. Human genes have been transferred to plants, such as tobacco, in efforts to produce large amounts of antibodies and enzymes to be used medically. A transgenic organism is one that contains genes from two different species.

Interferon is a naturally produced protein that fights viral infections. A single litre of bacterial culture that has had the gene for interferon inserted can produce the same amount of the protein as thousands of litres of blood in the human body. Bacteria-produced insulin has also become important in the treatment of diabetes. In agriculture, applications of genetic engineering include the development of plants with resistance to insect pests and disease.

Not everyone agrees that genetic engineering is a good thing. Some people want to stop all experiments with genetically modified organisms (GMOs). A few have resorted to direct action by destroying GM (genetically modified) crops. Many more campaigners have protested peacefully, like these.

Gene therapy

Humans have between 20,000 and 30,000 different genes. Genes are instructions coded in DNA to produce proteins, the molecules that help organize and direct every aspect of the way the body works. If a gene is defective, the consequences can be disastrous. About 4,000 genetic diseases have been identified. They are passed down from parent to child, generation after generation. Until very recently they have never been considered curable, but this may soon change.

Viral messengers

Gene therapy is a new branch of medicine that has been made possible by genetic engineering. Methods have been developed to take normal copies of human genes and give them to people who have inherited damaged genes. The "messengers" used to carry the healthy genes into the patient's cells are viruses.

Viruses are a very good way of delivering genes to cells. It is relatively easy to insert an additional gene into the viral DNA, producing a hybrid virus called a recombinant delivery vector. The virus itself is made harmless so that it cannot cause disease, but the genes it carries will be read and used just as if they were part of the host cell's own DNA. This technique involves taking white blood cells from a person with a genetic disease and then introducing a normal gene into the defective cell. The normal gene is delivered using a retrovirus, a type of virus that inserts its genes into the DNA of the target cell, introducing the properly functioning gene as it does so.

Developing therapies

Gene therapy is now being developed for the treatment of many hereditary diseases, including cystic fibrosis. In patients with this illness, a defective gene causes the production of mucus that is too thick to carry out its normal function of removing particles and bacteria from the airways. The thickened mucus clogs the airways, making breathing difficult. For cystic fibrosis, another type of virus, called an adenovirus, has been used as the carrier for the healthy gene.

Doctors Culver, Blaese, and French Anderson (from left to right) carried out the first successful treatment of a genetic disease using gene therapy.

Ashanthi DeSilva

The first human genetic disease to be treated by gene therapy was a form of severe combined immunodeficiency disease, or SCID. This illness affects children who are born without a type of white blood cell called T cells. Without T cells the immune system, our protection against disease, cannot work properly. One form of SCID is caused by a defective gene. A team of researchers at the National Institutes of Health in the United States used gene therapy to treat four-year-old Ashanthi DeSilva in 1990. Some of Ashanthi's cells were removed from her blood and exposed to the virus containing the healthy gene. The virus, which had been made harmless, invaded the cells and carried the gene with them into the blood cell DNA. They were then returned to her body. After a few treatments her immune system was almost totally normal. Ten years later, she was still doing well.

Extreme enzymes

Many industrial processes are carried out at high temperatures and pressures and involve the use of substances that are harmful to the environment. Biological substances are considered to be more environmentally "friendly" because they can be broken down naturally, but their use in industrial processes has been limited by their inability to withstand the harsh conditions that are involved.

Extremophiles

There are some micro-organisms that can flourish in surprisingly hostile environments. For example, some are found around undersea volcanic vents where the water temperature approaches boiling point. These are the extremophiles, members of a unique kingdom called the Archae. The extremophiles represent the most ancient forms of life on Earth. They appear to have evolved at a time when conditions on our planet were much harsher than they are now.

The Morning Glory hot spring in Yellowstone National Park. The colours are a result of the dissolved minerals and the bacteria that live there. Some of the cyanobacteria can tolerate temperatures of 165°C (329°F).

Extremozymes

The robust enzymes, or biological **catalysts**, that these bacteria employ in their essential life processes are sometimes called extreme enzymes or extremozymes. The unique properties of the extremozymes make them an attractive proposition for use in industry. For example, a bleaching enzyme produced by an extremophile found in the scalding springs of Yellowstone National Park in the United States could provide an alternative to chlorine for paper-whitening. A heat-tolerant extremozyme in commercial use has helped to increase the production of compounds called cyclodextrins from corn flour. These have many uses, including improving the uptake of medicines by the body, and reducing bitterness and unpleasant odours in foods and medicines.

Cold-lovers

Extremophiles are also found in very cold places. These are called psychrophiles, or cold-lovers. Manufacturers who need enzymes that work at low temperatures have become interested in psychrophile enzymes. They would be useful in industries such as food processing, where temperatures are kept low to avoid spoilage.

Biological washing

Alkali-tolerant extremophiles are found in soda lakes in such places as Egypt and the western United States. Detergent makers are particularly interested in their enzymes. Detergents must be able to cope with stains from food and this is best done by enzymes called proteases (which break down **proteins**) and lipases (which break down grease). Detergents tend to be highly alkaline, however, and this destroys ordinary proteases and lipases. Extremophile versions of these enzymes that can operate efficiently in heat or cold are now in use or being developed.

Home-grown extremozymes

Obtaining extremozymes in sufficient quantities can be difficult. One approach is to use genetic engineering to insert the gene for an extremozyme into a more easily grown bacterium such as *Escherichia coli*. This eliminates the need to obtain the bacteria from their extreme locations.

Biomining

Biomining makes use of micro-organisms that dissolve minerals out of rocks. By this method minerals can be obtained without the need for the heavy machinery used in other mining methods. Recovery rates have increased and operating costs decreased where biomining has been used.

Microbe miners

Biomining is not a new discovery. Two thousand years ago the Romans noticed that water running off the wastepile of one of their copper mines in Spain was blue with copper salts. They found ways to recover the copper but had no idea as to how the metal had been dissolved.

It was not until the mid-20th century that the bacterium *Thiobacillus ferrooxidans* was shown to be responsible. This bacterium gets energy by combining inorganic materials, such as sulphide-containing minerals, with oxygen. As part of their natural chemical processes, the bacteria release acids and other chemicals, which can wash metals out of ore.

Acid starter

Biomining is an inexpensive way to extract copper from ores where the metal is found in rocks that contain sulphur. The bacteria attack the ore, which is treated with sulphuric acid to get the process off to a good start. As the bacteria take the nutrients they need from the sulphur compounds, the copper is released and concentrated in a solution that can be collected. The metal is extracted from the solution, which is then recycled and used to prime the next batch of microbiominers.

Booming biomining

The copper industry was quick to put biomining to work. About 25 per cent of world copper production is based on biomining.

Raw copper ore is ground into slurry here before bacteria are used to separate the copper from the rock.

Gold diggers

Thiobacillus ferrooxidans is also being used successfully on gold-bearing ores. Low-grade gold ore often contains the metal bound up with sulphides, such as copper ore. Conventional extraction methods require roasting or high-pressure oxidation to burn off the sulphides before the gold is then extracted using cyanide. Using bacteria not only removes the need for these costly procedures, it can sometimes nearly double the rate of gold extraction.

Engineering biominers

In the future scientists may look at ways of genetically altering the bacteria to make them even more efficient. No doubt there will be objections to releasing genetically modified organisms into the environment in this way.

Oil wells, biofilms, and UMBs

Bacteria often form colonies called **biofilms**. A biofilm may contain billions upon billions of micro-organisms attached to a surface, which could be a rock, a piece of machinery, or even a tooth, as long as there is a plentiful supply of food. The bacteria produce a slimy coat that not only gives protection but also acts as a trap for food.

Ultra-micro bacterium

The other side of the bacterium's lifestyle is the ultra-micro bacterium (UMB). When food is scarce a bacterium can shut down most of its activities and shrink to about a third of its normal size. It can remain in this **dormant** state, perhaps for centuries, until conditions improve. If conditions improve sufficiently the dormant bacteria can form biofilms again.

Oil extraction

The oil industry is always keen to extract more oil from its wells. When an oil well is first drilled, about a third of the oil deposit will gush out simply because it is under pressure. Perhaps a third more can be recovered by pumping water into the well, to increase the pressure.

The Earth's deposits of oil and other minerals will not last for ever. Biofilms might enable us to make the most efficient use of these precious resources.

The final third is difficult to reach because the injected water leaks into rocks around the oil deposit, and oil gets stuck in the fine tubes and holes of the porous rocks.

Life in the depths

Scientists believe that the ability of bacteria to change between biofilms and UMBs may be put to good use. One way to plug the holes in the rocks around oil deposits is to use a biofilm. In the early 1990s, the American Department of Energy sampled for microbes while drilling for oil 2,440 metres (8,005 feet) below the surface. The researchers found that there was a surprisingly rich variety of bacteria in the oil wells.

Tiny spheres

All bacteria will go into the ultra-micro form when they are deprived of food. About 60 per cent become tiny smooth spheres as they do so. When faced with a leaky oil well, scientists can take samples of the bacteria in the well, looking for those that will form smooth shapes. These are then grown in the laboratory until they reach a very high concentration, something in the order of 500 billion bacteria per millilitre. Then they are deprived of food and made to enter the ultra-micro state. In this form they are shipped back to the oil well as a paste.

Bacteria in the borehole

At the well the bacteria paste is diluted and injected into the borehole. A rich food supply is then injected after them. Very rapidly the bacteria emerge from their dormant state and form a biofilm on the rocks that will block up all the holes and prevent leakage.

Dr Bill Costerton of Montana State University in the United States developed the scheme. He thinks that the method can be applied more generally, perhaps to contain polluted sites or to make harmful substances safe.

Anti-pollution microbes

Some types of groundwater-living microbes have been found to have the ability to consume and digest polluting chemicals. The micro-organisms use the pollutants as a source of food and energy, breaking them down in the process into byproducts such as water, carbon dioxide, methane, and hydrogen. This can bring the level of contamination back down to safe levels again.

Making a living

Micro-organisms such as bacteria have had millions of years and countless millions of generations in which to evolve a host of complex biochemical means of extracting a living from seemingly unlikely materials. Hugely diverse populations of bacteria exist below the Earth's surface that have the ability to break down many materials, both natural and artificial.

Bioremediation

Bioremediation is the name given to the use of biotechnology to clean up pollutants from the environment. Bioremediation technology can be applied to polluted ground without any soil being excavated. First, appropriate strains of bacteria that can be found in the contaminated area need to be identified. The bacteria are then cultured in a laboratory to bring their numbers up to the required level. The micro-organisms are then re-injected into the soil in the polluted area where they can get to work breaking down the pollutants.

The right bacteria for the job

One problem with bioremediation is that finding and successfully culturing suitable bacteria can be both costly and time consuming. Another is that it may take years for the bacteria to clean up the polluted area. Scientists are looking at ways of extracting the enzymes used by the bacteria to break down the pollutants. If these could be successfully produced in the laboratory it might be possible to treat the pollution problem directly, without the expense of maintaining a large microbe population.

Better biodigesters?

Bacteria can even take on chemical pollutants such as polychlorinated biphenyls that resist treatment by other means. Scientists hope to develop genetically engineered strains of bacteria that will biodigest multiple chemicals because most polluted areas are contaminated with more than one chemical. However, there would inevitably be resistance to the idea of introducing genetically engineered bacteria into the environment.

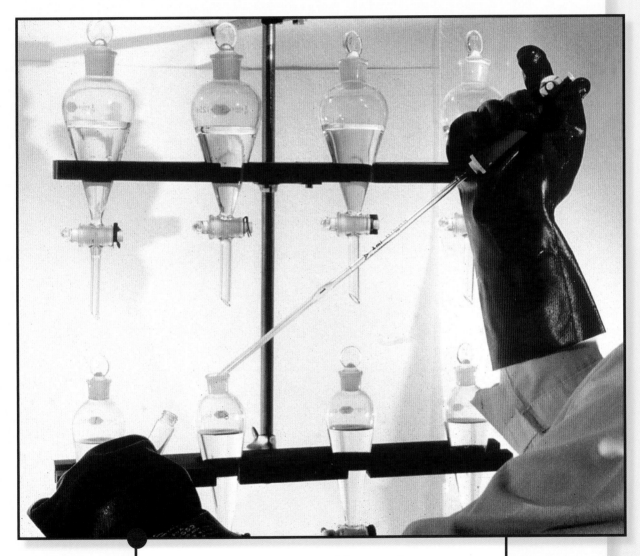

A laboratory technician adds microbes to a solution of toxic chemicals to observe how well the microbes break the chemicals down.

Glossary

aerated supplied with a gas, such as oxygen

alga(e) non-flowering single-celled plant, usually living in water

antibiotic substance produced by or obtained from certain bacteria or fungi that can be used to kill or inhibit the growth of disease-causing micro-organisms

bacteriophage virus that attacks a bacterium

bacterium (plural bacteria) any of a large group of single-celled organisms that have no organized nucleus

biofilm colony of billions of bacteria living on a surface that can provide them with water and nutrients. The biofilm colony produces a protective, slimy coat.

catalyst something that can change the rate of a chemical reaction without itself being altered in the reaction

cell the basic unit of life. Cells can exist as independent life forms, such as bacteria and protists, or form tissues in more complicated life forms, such as muscle cells and nerve cells in animals.

cholesterol substance found in the body that is an essential part of cell membranes. Cholesterol is produced by the liver and is also present in foods such as eggs, butter, and red meat. High cholesterol levels are thought to contribute to hardening of the arteries.

chromosome thread-like structures that become visible in the nucleus of a cell just before it divides. Chromosomes carry the genes that determine the characteristics of an organism.

coagulation transformation of a liquid into a soft, semi-solid mass

compound substance formed from two or more chemical elements

culture micro-organisms grown in the laboratory in a nutrient substance

cyanobacterium type of bacterium that is capable of photosynthesizing

disease agent organism, such as a bacterium, that can cause disease in another organism

DNA (deoxyribonucleic acid) the genetic material of almost all living things with the exception of some viruses. DNA consists of two long chains of nucleotides joined together in a double helix (a shape like a twisted ladder).

dormant temporarily inactive but able to be activated again at some point

ecosystem plants and animals in an area and the environment that affects them

enzyme type of protein that acts as a catalyst, altering the rate of a biochemical reaction

eutrophication process by which micro-organisms, such as bacteria and algae, grow in large numbers in water that is rich in nutrients, resulting in the death of other organisms as the micro-organisms use up the oxygen in the water

evolve in biology, to develop a characteristic over a period of time as a result of mutation and natural selection

ferment chemical breakdown of sugars using bacteria or yeasts in the absence of oxygen. Fermentation is used in baking bread and in making wine and beer.

filament fine, thread-like structure

fixation the act of fixing; in biology nitrogen fixing is the process by which nitrogen is converted into compounds that can be used by living things

fungus (plural fungi) any of a group of spore-producing organisms such as mushrooms and moulds

gene unit of heredity. A gene is a length of DNA and a number of genes are carried on a chromosome. A gene is a set of instructions for assembling a protein from amino acids.

glucose simplest form of sugar, produced by green plants and some other organisms by combining carbon dioxide and water in photosynthesis

heredity the passing of characteristics from parent to offspring by means of the genes that the offspring inherits

hybrid something that results from the combination of genetic material from two different species

inorganic describes something that is not produced by living things

microbe another name for a micro-organism

micro-organism any microscopic living thing, such as bacteria and protists

nitrates compounds of nitrogen in which each nitrogen atom is combined with three atoms of oxygen. Nitrates are absorbed by plants from the soil.

nucleic acids DNA and RNA. DNA encodes genetic information and RNA "reads" this information and translates it into protein production.

nutrient any nutritious substance found in food

oxidize combining of a substance with oxygen

parasite one organism living on another and benefiting without giving anything in return

photosynthesis process by which green plants and some micro-organisms make carbohydrates from carbon dioxide and water using the energy of sunlight

plasmid circular strand of DNA found in bacteria that is separate from the main chromosome DNA

pores minute openings, or tiny spaces in rock or soil

protein one of a group of complex organic molecules that perform a variety of essential tasks in living things, including providing structure and controlling the rates of chemical reactions

protist single-celled organism that is a member of the kingdom Protista

RNA (ribonucleic acid) found in different forms within cells, RNA is involved in the process by which the genetic code of DNA is translated into the production of proteins in the cell

symbiotic describes a close association between organisms of two different species that is of benefit to both

toxin poisonous substance produced by an organism such as a bacterium

virus infective particle, usually consisting of a molecule of nucleic acid in a protein coat

Further research

More Books to Read

Science Answers: Microlife, Anna Claybourne (Heinemann Library, 2005)

Micro World: Microscopic Life in Your Food, Brian Ward (Franklin Watts, 2006)

Microlife That Helps Us, Steve Parker (Raintree, 2006)

Using the Internet

Explore the Internet to find out more about the benefits of bacteria. You can use a search engine, such as www.yahooligans.com or www.google.com, and type in keywords such as *useful bacteria, antibiotics, bacteriophages*, or *genetic engineering*. These search tips will help you find useful websites more quickly:

* Know exactly what you want to find out about first.

* Use only a few important keywords in a search, putting the most relevant words first.

* Be precise. Only use names of people, places or things.

Index